All About Bees

by The Bug Collective

Table of Content

INTRODUCTION

Introduction to Bees

Are you ready to embark on an exciting journey into the fascinating world of bees? In this chapter, we will explore these incredible creatures, their importance in the natural world, and their intriguing behaviors. Whether you are a curious child or a curious child at heart, get ready to be amazed by the wondrous world of bees!

Bees are small insects that belong to the order Hymenoptera, which also includes ants and wasps. They are known for their distinctive black and yellow stripes, fuzzy bodies, and delicate wings. While there are over 20,000 known species of bees, we will focus on the most common ones found across the globe.

These buzzing creatures have captured the imaginations of people for centuries. From their intricate social structures to their role as diligent pollinators, bees are truly remarkable beings. But what makes them so special?

One of the most fascinating aspects of bees is their complex social hierarchy. In a bee colony, there is a queen bee, worker bees, and drones. The queen bee is the leader of the colony and is responsible for laying eggs. She is often larger than the other bees and has a distinct royal presence.

Worker bees, on the other hand, are female bees who do not lay eggs but perform crucial tasks within the colony. They are responsible for building and maintaining the hive, gathering nectar and pollen, and taking care of the larvae. From cleaning the hive to guarding its entrance, worker bees play a vital role in the functioning of the entire colony.

Drones, on the other hand, are male bees who exist solely for the purpose of mating with the queen bee. They do not have stingers and do not contribute to the daily tasks of the colony. Nevertheless, their existence is vital for the survival of the species.

But wait, here's a funny fact for you buzzing kids! Did you know that drones, the male bees, are often kicked out of the hive when they fulfill their purpose? It's like the strictest form of parenting; "Alright, boys, it's time to go now!" But don't feel too bad for the drones, they can still find food and shelter elsewhere.

Aside from their social dynamics, bees are also known for their unique method of communication. Through a dance-like movement known as the "waggle dance," bees can communicate important information to their fellow hive mates. Imagine if you had to do a dance to tell your friends where the tastiest ice cream shop is! Bees are truly talented dancers.

This dance indicates the direction and distance of a potential food source, enabling other bees to locate it easily. And speaking of food, bees have a sweet tooth just like us. They collect nectar from flowers, which they turn into honey. Honey is not only delicious, but it is also an important source of energy for the bees during colder months when flowers are scarce.

But perhaps the most critical role that bees play in our world is that of pollinators. As they move from flower to flower in search of nectar, bees inadvertently transfer pollen, allowing plants to reproduce. This process is responsible for the growth of fruits, vegetables, and flowers, making bees essential for agriculture and ecosystem balance.

Imagine a world without bees – we wouldn't have juicy apples, bright sunflowers, or yummy strawberries anymore! Bees are like little gardeners, helping plants grow and produce the fruits and vegetables we enjoy.

CHAPTER 1

The World of Bees

The world of bees is a fascinating and intricate one. These small creatures play a vital role in our ecosystem, and understanding their world can help us appreciate their importance even

.

Bees are found in almost every part of the world, except for the harsher climates of Antarctica and the extreme peaks of the Himalayas. They are most abundant in temperate regions, where the climate and floral resources are ideal for their survival.

One of the most incredible aspects of the world of bees is their social structure. Bees live in colonies, which consist of three main types of bees: the queen, drones, and worker bees. The queen bee is the ruler of the colony, responsible for laying eggs and ensuring the survival of the colony. Drones are male bees whose sole purpose is to mate with the queen, while worker bees are females responsible for various tasks such as collecting nectar, building and maintaining the hive, and caring for the young.

Bees are known for their remarkable ability to communicate. They use a complex language called the "waggle dance" to communicate the location of food sources to other bees in the colony. By performing a carefully choreographed dance, a bee can convey information about the direction and distance of a food source, allowing other bees to navigate and find the riches of pollen and nectar.

The world of bees is also a world of hard work. Bees are diligent and tireless workers, visiting hundreds of flowers each day to collect nectar and pollen. They play a crucial role in the pollination of plants, ensuring the reproduction and survival of countless species. Without bees, our environment would suffer, and the production of many fruits and vegetables would significantly decline.

But let's not forget the funny side of bees! Bees have some amusing behaviors that can entertain both kids and adults. Did you know that bees have a great sense of humor? Well, maybe not intentionally, but there are some funny situations they find themselves in. Sometimes bees accidentally bump into each other while flying, creating a mini "bumble" - a playful name for a little bee collision. It's like a bee version of bumper cars! And have you ever seen a bee dance? It's not the most graceful dance moves you'll ever see, but it sure is entertaining! They wiggle and waggle their bodies as if showing off their own unique choreography.

However, bees also face numerous challenges in their world. Factors such as habitat loss, pesticide use, climate change, and diseases pose significant threats to bee populations worldwide. It is important for us to understand and address these challenges to ensure the preservation of these invaluable creatures.

To help protect bees and make their world a better place, we can take simple actions. We can create bee-friendly gardens by planting flowers that provide them with nectar and pollen. Avoiding the use of harmful pesticides in our gardens also helps keep bees safe. Additionally, supporting local beekeepers and their honey products can contribute to the preservation of bee populations.

In conclusion, the world of bees is a marvel to behold. These small insects play a critical role in our environment, pollinating plants and contributing to the diversity of our ecosystems. Without bees, our world would be a very different place. By learning more about the world of bees, we can appreciate their importance and work towards protecting and conserving them for future generations. So, let's embrace the funny and fascinating aspects of bees while also taking action to safeguard their habitat and ensure a world filled with buzzing joy for generations to come!

CHAPTER 2

Anatomy of a Bee

As we delve into the fascinating world of bees, it is essential to explore the intricate anatomy that makes these incredible creatures function. Bees possess a unique set of physical features that allow them to perform their incredibly important role in our ecosystem. So, let's take a closer look at the anatomy of a bee, and get ready for some amazing and even funny facts!

The body of a bee is divided into three main regions: the head, thorax, and abdomen. Each part plays a crucial role in the bee's survival and functionality. Let's dive in!

Starting with the head, bees have two large compound eyes that give them excellent vision. These compound eyes are made up of thousands of tiny hexagonal lenses that give them a segmented appearance. It's like they have superpowers to see the world in a unique way. Just imagine if we had so many tiny eyes on our face, we would look quite hilarious, wouldn't we?

In addition to their compound eyes, bees also possess three simple eyes called ocelli. Positioned on the top of their heads, these small eyes may seem insignificant, but they can detect changes in light intensity, which helps bees navigate, even during cloudy days. It's like having their own built-in weather forecast! Talk about being prepared for any situation.

Now let's move on to the mouthparts. Bees have a long, straw-like organ called a proboscis. It's like they have their own built-in drinking straw! With this amazing tool, bees can reach deep into flowers to collect nectar. But do you know the cool part? When they are not using it, they can actually fold their proboscis and tuck it away like a hidden secret weapon. It's like they're part samurai and part party magician!

As we venture into the thorax, the middle region of the bee's body, we find their six legs, which are pretty remarkable. Have you ever seen a bee carrying bags of pollen on its legs? Well, those bags are called pollen baskets, and they are like built-in backpacks that allow bees to bring back pollen to their hive. It's like they're bees running errands for their colony, equipped with stylish and efficient storage solutions. Talk about multi-tasking!

And of course, let's not forget about the wings! Bees have two pairs of wings that enable them to fly. But here's something amusing: their wings beat at an amazingly fast rate, around 200 beats per second! If we tried to flap our arms that quickly, we would look like a very dizzy superhero attempting a not-so-super takeoff. It's a good thing we have bees to do the flying for us!

Last but certainly not least, we come to the abdomen, the back end of a bee. This is where all the important stuff happens! Bees have a sophisticated digestive system that helps them break down the nectar they collect into honey. They also have a reproductive system that allows the queen bee to lay eggs and continue the cycle of life for their hive. Oh, and let's not forget about the stinger! Bees have a stinger that can be quite funny (unless you get stung, of course). Only female bees possess a stinger, and it's like their superhero power, but they can only use it once. After stinging, the stinger detaches from the bee's body, leaving them in a bit of a predicament. It's like a prank with a twist, reminding us to respect these tiny but mighty creatures.

The anatomy of a bee is truly marvelous, and exploring it brings a whole new level of amazement and fun. These incredible creatures have evolved unique features over millions of years, and by understanding their anatomy, we can develop a deeper appreciation for the wonders of nature.

So, next time you encounter a buzzing bee, take a moment to marvel at its intricate and sometimes funny anatomy. Remember, they are superhero insects playing their important roles in our world, bringing joy and pollinating the flowers that surround us. With every flap of their wings, bees remind us that even the tiniest creatures can have the greatest impact.

CHAPTER 3

BEE

The Life Cycle of a Bee

Bees are amazing creatures that undergo a fascinating life cycle filled with incredible transformations and important milestones. In this chapter, we will explore the intricate stages of a bee's life in even greater detail – with a sprinkle of funny for kids! Get ready to dive into the buzzing world of bees and discover the secrets behind their extraordinary journey.

Stage 1: Egg-citing Beginnings

Let's start our journey at the beginning – the egg stage. Just like how we start with a blank page when writing a story, the queen bee lays thousands of tiny, inconspicuous eggs. These eggs are so small that you might need a bee-sized magnifying glass to spot them. Imagine being so tiny that even the smallest Lego piece would look gigantic to you! It's like they're hiding a secret message and need to leave their markings behind in tiny font!

Stage 2: Larva

Lah-Lah-Land Once the eggs hatch, out come the larvae! At this stage, they are like little adventurers embarking on a thrilling journey. These legless creatures need lots of energy to grow, just like when you need to eat your fruits and veggies to become big and strong! The worker bees take care of the larvae, providing them with a special treat called royal jelly. It's like a superfood smoothie for baby bees, packed with all the nutrients they need to grow quickly! It's as if the worker bees are their personal chefs, whipping up yummy meals like a 5-star restaurant!

Stage 3: Pupa Party

Now, hold onto your honey jars because things are about to get really interesting! After their larval adventures, the bees transform into pupae. It's during this stage that they undergo a magical metamorphosis! Just like a superhero putting on a cape and mask, the developing bees wrap themselves in a cozy cocoon and stay inside a special wax cell. Inside this hidden sanctuary, their bodies go through incredible changes, almost like a caterpillar turning into a butterfly! It's like having a superhero costume fitting session, with snug cocoons tailored just for them!

Stage 4: Adult Bee Brilliance

After patiently waiting inside their cocoons, the bees emerge as fully-formed adults. It's like they're wearing a brand-new bee suit, all fresh and ready to take on the world! At first, they might seem a little soft and pale, but once they meet the air, they quickly transform into harder and darker versions of themselves. They are now worker bees, and their to-do list is buzzing with important tasks for the colony.

From collecting nectar and pollen to making honey and beeswax, these worker bees keep the hive thriving. It's like they're marathon runners, buzzing from flower to flower, gathering precious resources for their colony like superheroes on a mission! On top of that, they take care of the next generation, making sure the larvae are well-fed and nurtured. It's like they have a superhero secret identity, blending seamlessly into the hive while still performing extraordinary feats! Oh, and let's not forget about the queen bees! Some lucky larvae receive a special diet that transforms them into royalty.

Stage 3: Pupa Party

Now, hold onto your honey jars because things are about to get really interesting! After their larval adventures, the bees transform into pupae. It's during this stage that they undergo a magical metamorphosis! Just like a superhero putting on a cape and mask, the developing bees wrap themselves in a cozy cocoon and stay inside a special wax cell. Inside this hidden sanctuary, their bodies go through incredible changes, almost like a caterpillar turning into a butterfly! It's like having a superhero costume fitting session, with snug cocoons tailored just for them!

Stage 4: Adult Bee Brilliance

After patiently waiting inside their cocoons, the bees emerge as fully-formed adults. It's like they're wearing a brand-new bee suit, all fresh and ready to take on the world! At first, they might seem a little soft and pale, but once they meet the air, they quickly transform into harder and darker versions of themselves. They are now worker bees, and their to-do list is buzzing with important tasks for the colony.

From collecting nectar and pollen to making honey and beeswax, these worker bees keep the hive thriving. It's like they're marathon runners, buzzing from flower to flower, gathering precious resources for their colony like superheroes on a mission! On top of that, they take care of the next generation, making sure the larvae are well-fed and nurtured. It's like they have a superhero secret identity, blending seamlessly into the hive while still performing extraordinary feats!

Oh, and let's not forget about the queen bees! Some lucky larvae receive a special diet that transforms them into royalty. They become future queens, destined to rule their own colonies someday! It's like a bee version of "The Bachelor" or "The Bachelorette," but without the fancy dresses or roses. Imagine a hive full of little crown-wearing bees, deliberating the honeycomb bachelor and bachelorette style!

In conclusion, the life cycle of a bee is a true marvel. These tiny creatures go through an extraordinary journey from egg to adult, undergoing significant transformations along the way. The intricate balance of their colony and their roles in pollination make bees essential to our ecosystem. So next time you see a buzzing bee, remember all the adventures it went through in its life cycle and give it a little bee-inspired cheer. "Bee" amazing, little bees! Keep buzzing with joy and laughter as you pollinate the world with your endless cuteness and hard work!

CHAPTER 4

CLASSIFATTION
CENTER

Classification of a Bee

Classification is an essential part of understanding the natural world and the diverse species that inhabit it. Bees, being one of the most crucial creatures on Earth, have their own unique classification system. We'll bee learning some fascinating bee facts and having a bee-utiful time. So put on your imaginary bee costumes and let's get buzzing!

1. Introduction to Bee Classification:

Bee classification is like sorting a candy jar into different types of delicious treats. It helps us understand and categorize bees based on their shared traits. Bees belong to the order Hymenoptera, which also includes wasps and ants. This order is like a big family reunion, with all three buzzing relatives coming together.

2. Families of Bees:

Apidae Family: This family is like the honeybee hive at a bee party – it's the largest and bee-loud family within the bee order. It includes honeybees, bumblebees, carpenter bees, and sweat bees. They might have different taste preferences, but they all love to boogie on flowers and spread sweet honey magic.

Megachilidae Family: These bees are like the superheroes of the bee world. They're known as mason bees, leafcutter bees, and carder bees because they build nests using plant materials. Just like superheroes wearing their capes, these bees use leaves or resin to create their bee-tiful homes.

Halictidae Family: Picture bees in sweatbands chilling in a trendy gym. These are the sweat bees, and they are certainly buzzing with energy! They are attracted to human perspiration, and you might spot them enjoying a workout near you. Don't worry, they won't make you smell like a flower gym!

Andrenidae Family: These bees are shy little miners, like the ones searching for gold nuggets. Andrenidae bees, fondly called mining bees, are solitary ground-nesting bees. They like digging little burrows in gardens and meadows, living their busy lives out of sight.

Colletidae Family: Let's not forget about the polyester bees! No, they don't wear polyester clothes, but they use a special water-resistant secretion to make their nests. They are known for their diversity of lifestyles, from solitary to communal bees. It's like having bees with different room-sharing preferences!

Melittidae Family: It's time to meet the bee artists! Melittidae bees, also called plasterer bees, are known for their intricate nest construction. They create cell partitions made of secreted waterproof substances. It's like sculpting with nature's materials!

3. Key features used in Bee Classification:

Body structure: Bees have their own unique sense of style. They have robust, hairy bodies that are perfect for collecting pollen. Imagine bees with tiny hairbrushes collecting all the pollen they can find, creating trendy fur coats for themselves.

Mouthparts and Tongue Length: Bees have a special sweet tooth, but they need help getting to their sugary snacks. That's where their proboscis, or long tongue, comes in handy. Some bees have short tongues to sip nectar from shallow flowers, while others have long tongues to reach into deep and tubular flowers. It's like having different types of straws for their favorite drinks!

Social Structure: Bees have their own bee-lievable communities. Some bees, like the friendly carpenter bees, enjoy living alone, while others, like the honeybees, prefer living together in organized colonies. In these bee-tastic communities, every bee has a special job to do – from gathering nectar to guarding the hive. It's all about teamwork!

4. Bee Species Diversity:

Hold onto your imaginary bee antennas! There are over 20,000 different bee species buzzing around the world. From the teeny-tiny stingless bees, which are like the pixies of the bee world, to the mighty carpenter bees, each species has its own superpowers. They come in all shapes, sizes, and colors – like a buzzing rainbow party!

Importance of Classification: Understanding bee classification helps us appreciate the bee-mazing diversity in our ecosystems. It allows scientists, beekeepers, and bee enthusiasts to study, conserve, and protect these little buzzing heroes. So let's join forces and protect our bee friends, because they truly make the world a sweeter and more colorful place!

CHAPTER 5

Bee Habitats

Bee habitats are buzzing with diversity and can be found in various ecosystems around the world. These habitats provide bees with the necessary resources for survival, including food, shelter, and suitable nesting sites. So, let's put on our adventure hats and explore the enchanting world of bee habitats and the unique characteristics they offer.

1. Forests:

Ah, the magical realm of forests, where bees flit among the towering trees and vibrant underbrush. Many bee species thrive in these woodland wonderlands, where they can find a bountiful array of flowering plants. From dainty wildflowers to majestic floral blooms, forests provide a banquet of nectar and pollen sources for bees. Hollow trees and fallen logs act as cozy bee hotels, offering ideal nesting sites for cavity-nesting bees. It's like a forest bed-andbreakfast for these busy pollinators!

But did you know that bees in the forest have a secret talent for rhythmic dancing? Yes, it's true! These industrious little creatures perform a waggle dance to communicate the location of rich floral resources to their fellow bees. It's their version of a bee boogie, and they're always in perfect sync!

2. Meadows and Grasslands:

Let's frolic in the open grassy landscapes, meadows, and prairies, where bees are busy as little bee-lls. These habitats are like colorful tapestries, woven with an abundance of wildflowers and flowering grasses. Buzzing with activity, meadows are like the bee equivalent of a sweet shop, serving up delectable nectar and pollen treats. Among the buzzing visitors, bumblebees and solitary ground-nesting bees are often spotted, adding their unique touch to this picture-perfect meadow paradise.

Interestingly, bees in meadows have a great sense of fashion sense. They collect colorful pollen grains to bring back to their nests, making them look like they're wearing vibrant polka-dotted pants. It's a fashion statement that only bees can pull off and adds a touch of whimsy to their already busy lives.

3. Wetlands:

Prepare to get your feet wet as we venture into the watery wonderland of wetlands. Marshes, swamps, and bogs may sound squishy, but they play host to a whole cast of bees that thrive in these specialized habitats. Imagine a colorful bouquet of wetland plants, each bloom providing a rich source of nectar and pollen for bees. Bees adapted to this sometimes boggy neighborhood play a crucial role in pollinating these plant species, lending a helping wing to the overall health of the ecosystem.

Did you know that wetland bees are fantastic acrobats? They navigate through the dense vegetation with ease, performing mid-air somersaults and aerial flips that would make even the most skilled circus performers envious. It's their way of showcasing their flying skills while collecting precious resources for their colony. Truly the daredevils of the bee world!

4. Gardens and Urban Spaces:

As we flit into the buzzing world of gardens, parks, and green spaces within cities, we discover that even concrete jungles can be enchanting. Bees have learned to adapt and find refuge amidst the hustle and bustle of urban environments. Among the flower beds and ornamental trees, they discover a secret treasure trove of nectar and pollen. These gardens become a grand banquet hall, with bees buzzing from one floral feast to another. And for urban bees looking for a place to rest their wings, specially designed bee hotels provide a five-star experience in the heart of the city.

Urban bees have a unique sense of style. They love to accessorize their nests with bits of shiny and colorful trash they find in the city. From discarded candy wrappers to discarded jewelry, their nests are a quirky mix of nature and urban flair. Who knew bees were such fashion-forward decorators?

5. Farmland:

Welcome to the countryside, where the scent of freshly tilled soil mingles with the hum of bees working their magic. As we explore the agricultural landscapes, we find that bees face both challenges and opportunities in these vast fields of crops. The rows of uniform crops may not provide a diverse menu for bees, but fear not, for colorful wildflowers and uncultivated spaces pepper the outskirts of farmland. These patches of natural beauty attract bees like magnets, offering a delightful bounty of flowers to satisfy their cravings. Through the integration of thoughtful conservation practices, such as planting cover crops and maintaining hedgerows, farmers and bee friends work together to create a buzzworthy habitat for these industrious pollinators.

Farmland bees are the ultimate travel enthusiasts. They embark on epic journeys, flying from one field to another in search of the best flowers. They might as well be called "bees-on-wings," as they explore vast expanses, collecting nectar like souvenirs from each stop along the way. Their adventurous spirit and knack for exploration make them the Indiana Joneses of the bee world!

6. Deserts:

Brace yourself for a sandy adventure into the deserts, where bees have found ingenious ways to dance among the cacti and sand dunes. These hardy bees have evolved to cope with extreme temperatures and limited water availability. Their survival depends on desert-adapted plant species that bloom during brief periods after rainfall, creating a desert oasis of colorful blooms. Bees dart in and out, sipping nectar from these delicately prepared desert delicacies. Sand dunes, rock crevices, and burrows become their secret hideaways, providing shelter from the scorching sun and harsh desert winds.

Desert bees are the true treasure hunters of the bee world. They have developed a remarkable ability to detect the faint scent of blooming flowers hidden amidst the arid sands, becoming nature's own metal detectors. These diligent seekers of floral riches navigate through the vast desert expanse, never giving up on the promise of a sweet reward. They truly embody the motto, "The desert is full of hidden wonders, and I'll find them!"

Now, with this newfound knowledge, we can appreciate the intricate relationship between bees and their remarkable habitats. It encourages us to take action in protecting and preserving these vital ecosystems, for it is in these habitats that bees thrive, weaving their magical web of pollination and helping to sustain life on our beautiful planet. So let's bee-ware and show the bees some love!

CHAPTER 6

Bee Behavior

Bees are fascinating creatures that constantly buzz with excitement and exhibit a wide range of behaviors, from their communication within the hive to their foraging habits. This chapter will take you on a deeper dive into the wondrous world of bee behavior, shedding light on their intricate social interactions, instincts, and a few quirky facts that will have you giggling like a bee!

One of the most delightful and whimsical behaviors of bees is their ability to communicate through a complex and comical dance known as the waggle dance. Can you imagine bees having their own secret language? Well, honeybees indeed do! When a foraging bee discovers a delectable food source, it performs an energetic dance inside the hive. It waggles, shakes, and moves in precise patterns to convey vital information to its hive mates. It's like their very own bee DJ mixing dance moves to spell out directions to the best flowers in town! Imagine if human communication was as entertaining as bee dance-offs!

As we explore the bustling bee community within the hive, let's take a closer look at the heart of the colony – the queen bee. With her majestic crown, she reigns supreme, laying eggs and maintaining harmony within the buzzing kingdom. She's like the queen bee of the insect world, with a dedicated royal court of worker bees ready to cater to her every need. It's a high-stakes game of thrones, but with honey and pollen instead of crowns and scepters!

Meanwhile, let's not forget about the worker bees, the unsung heroes of the hive. These multi-talented ladies take on a myriad of roles, juggling tasks with the grace of a bee ballet. They nurse the brood, gently feeding the growing larvae, and they build and repair the hive, ensuring a safe and cozy home. But that's not all – they also collect nectar and pollen, transforming themselves into pollen-carrying superheroes with a mission to feed the colony. And, of course, they're responsible for making the sweet and golden honey that tickles our taste buds. It's safe to say that worker bees are the ultimate multitaskers, buzzing around with a neverending to-do list!

Now, let's venture into the world of the male bees, the drones. Picture them as the honeybee version of laid-back slackers hanging around the hive, sipping bee juice and waiting for opportunities to socialize. Their primary, and some might say privileged, purpose is to mate with the queen bee, grabbing their version of a "golden ticket." But beware, my young readers! Once their mission is complete, the drones are unceremoniously evicted from the hive, left to wander aimlessly or meet their fate. It's as if being a drone includes a one-way ticket to the bee hotel with no chance of a return trip! Talk about a buzzkill!

When it comes to teamwork, bees are the epitome of cooperation and efficiency. They work together with a precision that could rival the most intricate choreography. Each bee knows its role and carries out its tasks diligently, contributing to the overall success of the colony. There's no room for laziness in the world of bees! If bees were human, they would certainly be the busiest worker bees among us, inspiring us to put on our buzz-worthy work ethic!

While bees are exceptional workers, they also possess remarkable skills in navigation and orientation. Picture a bee with a built-in compass and a nose better than any bloodhound!

Bees have an extraordinary ability to remember and recognize landmarks, allowing them to find their way back to the hive after exploration. They're like tiny aviators with an impeccable GPS system in their fuzzy little heads. To top it off, bees have a keen sense of smell that helps them locate the sweetest flowers with nectar and pollen. With this un-bee-lievable combo of talents, they become the superheroes of pollination, ensuring plants thrive and bloom.

Now, it's time to buzz on to a rather stinging topic – defense! While bees are generally peaceful creatures, they will protect their hive with unwavering determination if a threat is sensed. Think of it as a bee martial arts showdown! Their defense mechanism, known as stinging, is both fascinating and, well, a little prickly. The bee stinger, a modified ovipositor, releases venom upon use, causing discomfort and, unfortunately, the end of the bee's life. It's a reminder to show respect and admire bees from a safe distance, appreciating their brave dedication to safeguarding their home.

In recent years, there has been a growing concern about the declining bee populations worldwide. This has sparked a frenzy of beekeepers, scientists, and even superhero gardeners working tirelessly to understand bee behavior. They seek insights into the factors contributing to bee decline, such as habitat loss, pesticide exposure, and climate change. Saving the bees has become a real mission where each of us can play a buzz-tastic role!

Whether you're fascinated by the enchanting waggle dance, amused by the bustling hive community, or in awe of the impressive navigation skills and teamwork of bees, their behavior is a true marvel to explore.

Through observation and study, we continue to unlock the mysteries of these extraordinary creatures and develop a deeper appreciation for their vital role in our ecosystems. So, put on your bee-sized detective goggles and embark on the bee-havior adventure of a lifetime! Just make sure to pack your sense of humor because bees are nature's little comedians, turning their buzzing world into a honey-filled playground of laughter and amazement!

CHAPTER 7

The Benefits of Bees

Bees are incredible creatures that play a vital role in our ecosystem. While they may seem small and insignificant, they provide us with a wide range of benefits that are often overlooked. In this chapter, we will delve even deeper into the remarkable ways bees positively impact our lives.

1. Pollination:

One of the most important benefits of bees is their role as pollinators. As bees move from flower to flower, they inadvertently transfer pollen, allowing plants to reproduce and produce fruits, vegetables, and nuts. Without bees, many of our favorite foods would not exist. From apples and blueberries to almonds and avocados, bees are like nature's little matchmakers, ensuring plants can make sweet love and bear the fruits (quite literally) of their labor.

But did you know that bees have some fascinating tricks up their sleeves? Bees have an amazing ability called "buzz pollination." Some flowers, like tomatoes and blueberries, require a specific buzzing frequency to release their pollen. Bees, being the smarty-pants they are, know exactly how to vibrate their flight muscles to create the perfect buzz and shake loose that precious pollen. It's like they're giving flowers their own little shake of encouragement!

2. Biodiversity:

Bees not only pollinate crops but also aid in the reproduction of wild plants. By facilitating the cross-pollination of various species, bees contribute to maintaining biodiversity in our ecosystems. The diversity of plants, in turn, supports a healthy and balanced environment for other wildlife and helps to sustain habitats.

Did you know that bees have been around for millions of years? They have evolved alongside flowering plants and have formed intricate partnerships with them. Some flowers even have special adaptations like long, tubular shapes or unique colors that attract specific types of bees. It's like a beautiful dance of coevolution between bees and flowers, with each side benefiting from the other's existence.

3. Honey Production:

Bees are expert honey makers. They collect nectar from flowers and transform it into the golden liquid we know and love. Honey has been a precious resource for humans for thousands of years. Apart from being a delicious natural sweetener, honey also offers numerous health benefits. It contains antioxidants, antibacterial properties, and can soothe coughs and sore throats.

Have you ever wondered why honey never spoils? Well, bees are clever chemists! When bees make honey, they remove most of the water content, which helps prevent spoilage. Additionally, honey has low pH and contains natural enzymes that create an inhospitable environment for bacteria and other microorganisms. It's like Mother Nature's magic potion of sweetness and preservation!

4. Beeswax and Propolis:

Beeswax is another valuable substance produced by bees. It is used to build their hive and create honeycomb cells, providing a safe home for the colony. Beeswax is also used by humans to make candles, cosmetics, and furniture polish, among other things. Propolis, a resinous substance collected by bees from tree buds, has antibacterial and antiviral properties. It is used by bees to seal their hive and protect it from pathogens. Humans have also found medicinal applications for propolis, using it in various health products and even for medical treatment.

Beeswax is like the construction material of the bee world! It's not only strong and durable but also waterproof. Beeswax is made by young bees, who chew up honey and combine it with special gland secretions to create wax flakes. They then mold these flakes into perfectly hexagonal honeycomb cells, displaying an awe-inspiring example of mathematical genius in nature.

And have you ever wondered how bees gather propolis? Well, they are like little tree scrapers! Bees collect sticky resins from tree buds and mix it with their own enzymes to make propolis. It's like their very own healing ointment, protecting their hive from unwanted intruders and maintaining the hygiene within.

5. Research and Science:

Bees have become a subject of great interest for scientists and researchers. Studying their behavior, communication, and social systems has shed light on complex biological processes and provided insights into human society. Bees have inspired innovations in robotics and technology, with scientists developing drones that mimic their flight patterns and hive structures.

Their unique abilities have even influenced architecture, where bee-inspired designs optimize space and energy efficiency.

Scientists have also discovered some interesting things about bee communication. Bees use a special dance called the "waggle dance" to communicate information about food sources to their hive mates. But did you know that bees can also remember human faces? In some experiments, researchers would wear differentcolored hats, and the bees could recognize which ones had a sugar reward. It's like having a personal fan club with wings!

6. Ecosystem Services:

Bees are considered key contributors to the ecosystem services provided by nature. By pollinating plants, they ensure the continuation of many vital habitats and food chains. The preservation of these ecosystems is crucial for maintaining biodiversity, improving air quality, and supporting climate regulation. Bees indirectly contribute to our well-being by maintaining the overall health and balance of our planet. Bees are nature's unsung heroes, working tirelessly to keep our ecosystems humming along. They not only provide us with food and resources but also ensure the survival of countless other species on Earth. Next time you see a bee buzzing by, take a moment to appreciate the incredible benefits these tiny creatures bring to our world. And remember, we owe a big "thank you" to our bee friends for all the sweetness they bring into our lives!

CHAPTER 8

Bees and the Environment

Bees are extraordinary creatures that have a special place in the natural world. Did you know that these buzzing superheroes not only produce honey but also help the environment in many ways? Let's dive deeper into the magical world of bees and discover the fascinating ways they play a vital role in keeping our planet healthy and happy.

One of the most amazing things about bees is their remarkable ability to pollinate plants. When bees fly from flower to flower, they unintentionally transfer pollen from the male parts of a flower to the female parts of another. This process is called pollination, and it plays a vital role in plant reproduction. Without bees and other pollinators, many plants wouldn't be able to produce fruits, vegetables, or even seeds. Can you imagine a world without delicious strawberries, juicy watermelons, or beautiful flowers? Thanks to bees, our world is bursting with colors, tastes, and delightful scents.

But the bee-power doesn't stop there! Bees also help to maintain a delicate balance in ecosystems. When bees pollinate plants, those plants provide important resources for other animals in their habitats. For example, birds may build their nests in the trees that bees pollinate, while butterflies and beetles may feast on the nectar from flowers bees have visited. This interconnected web of life is not only fascinating but crucial for maintaining biodiversity.

However, bees face challenges that put their well-being at risk. One of the biggest concerns for our buzzing friends is pesticides. Pesticides are chemicals used to protect crops from harmful bugs, but sadly, they can also harm bees.

When bees come into contact with these chemicals, it can affect their health, making it harder for them to survive and perform their essential pollination duties. That's why it's important for farmers and gardeners to adopt organic and bee-friendly practices, so bees can play safely in their fields.

Another problem for bees is habitat loss. As cities grow and more land is used for agriculture, the places where bees can build their homes and find food become limited. Bees need a variety of flowers to gather nectar and pollen from, as well as safe places to build their hives. But fear not! Each of us can be a superhero for bees by planting bee-friendly gardens with lots of colorful flowers and creating cozy bee hotels or providing them with bee boxes as homes. It's like having a vacation resort for bees right in our own backyard!

Climate change is another serious issue affecting our buzzing buddies. Rising temperatures and changing weather patterns can disrupt the timing of when plants bloom. Imagine if flowers bloomed too early and there were no bees around to help pollinate them? This could lead to fewer fruits, vegetables, and seeds, which would impact not only bees but also the animals and people who rely on them. Taking action to combat climate change, like reducing our carbon footprint and supporting renewable energy, can make a big difference in the lives of bees and the planet.

Now, let's sprinkle a little fun bee trivia for our little readers: Did you know that a group of bees is called a colony? And just like any other society, bees have different jobs within their colony. The queen bee, who is the mother of all the other bees, lays eggs and ensures the colony thrives. Worker bees, the ones we usually see buzzing around, gather nectar and pollen, build and protect the hive, and even take care of the baby bees (larvae). Male bees, known as drones, don't have stingers and their main purpose is to mate with the queen bee. How fascinating is that?

So next time you see a bee buzzing around, take a moment to appreciate these tiny yet mighty creatures. From pollinating plants to helping maintain a balanced ecosystem, bees are true environmental superheroes. Let's protect their habitats, say no to harmful pesticides, and spread the word about the incredible impact these little creatures have on our world. Together, we can ensure a bright and buzzing future for bees and the environment!

(Note: If you would like a specific topic or aspect of bees to be explored in more depth, please let me know, and I will be happy to provide additional information.)

CHAPTER 9

Bees in Human History

Throughout history, bees have played a significant role in shaping human civilization. From ancient civilizations to modern societies, bees have been intertwined with human culture, economy, and even spirituality. Let's delve into the fascinating history of bees and their impact on humanity.

The earliest evidence of humans interacting with bees dates back to ancient times. The Egyptians were one of the first civilizations to document their relationship with bees. They revered bees for their ability to produce honey, which was considered a precious and valuable commodity. Honey was not only used as a food source but also for medicinal purposes, embalming, and even as an offering to the gods. In fact, honey was found in ancient Egyptian tombs, illustrating its significance in their belief system.

The Greeks also held bees in high regard. They linked bees with the gods and saw them as messengers between the mortal and divine realms. The renowned philosopher Aristotle even studied bee behavior and wrote extensively about their societal structure and organization, noting their remarkable ability to work together for the greater good of their hive.

Moving forward in history, bees continued to be prominently featured. During the Middle Ages in Europe, beekeeping became a respected profession and an important source of income for many. Beekeepers played a vital role in supplying honey, beeswax, and other bee-related products to their communities. In fact, beekeeping became so integral to the economies of certain regions that laws were enacted to protect bee colonies and regulate the beekeeping industry.

Bees also influenced art and literature throughout the centuries. In ancient mythology, bees were associated with goddesses like Aphrodite and Demeter, symbolizing fertility and abundance. This symbolism carried into art and literature, where bees often represented industriousness, harmony, and prosperity. From ancient Greek poetry to Renaissance paintings, bees featured prominently, leaving an indelible mark on the cultural heritage of various civilizations.

As exploration and trade expanded in the 16th and 17th centuries, bees made their way to the Americas. European settlers introduced honeybees to the New World, where they thrived in their new environments. Bees played a crucial role in pollinating crops, leading to agricultural advancements and increased food production. The discovery of this natural pollination process greatly enhanced human agriculture and ensured the abundance of various crops.

In modern times, the importance of bees in human history continues to be recognized. However, with the rise of industrialization and the use of pesticides, bees face numerous challenges. The decline in bee populations and the phenomenon of colony collapse disorder have raised concerns globally. Initiatives have emerged to protect bees and raise awareness about their crucial role in maintaining biodiversity and ensuring food security.

Now, let's delve deeper into the incredible societal structure and organization of bees. Within a beehive, thousands of worker bees, a queen, and a few drones all form a complex society. Each member has a specific role and responsibility.

Worker bees, which are all female, perform numerous tasks to ensure the survival of the hive. They collect nectar and pollen, build and repair the hive, tend to the queen, and care for the brood. Did you know that worker bees have specialized pollen baskets on their hind legs? These baskets, called corbiculae, allow them to carry large amounts of pollen back to the hive.

Interestingly, worker bees are all sisters, born from the same queen, and they share more genetic material with each other than they do with their own offspring. This unique familial bond strengthens their cooperation and their dedication to the hive's well-being.

The queen bee is the heart of the hive. She is the mother of all the worker bees and drones, laying up to 2,000 eggs per day during peak season. Her pheromones keep the hive functioning smoothly, preventing worker bees from reproducing and maintaining harmony among the colony. If the queen bee dies or becomes too weak, the worker bees will take immediate action to raise a new queen by selecting a few larvae and feeding them a special diet called "royal jelly." This jelly triggers their development into queens, ensuring the hive's survival.

Drones, on the other hand, are male bees whose sole purpose is to mate with a queen. They do not have stingers, and their role is short-lived. After mating, drones die, and those remaining within the hive during the winter are often expelled by the worker bees to conserve resources.

Bees communicate with each other through a unique dance called the waggle dance. When a forager bee returns to the hive after finding a valuable food source, she performs this intricate dance to inform other workers of the direction, distance, and quality of the discovered resource. By varying the speed, angle, and duration of their dance, bees can communicate valuable information to their fellow foragers, ensuring efficient utilization of available resources.

Aside from their vital role in pollination, bees also produce honey, which has been consumed by humans for thousands of years. Bees collect nectar from flowers using their long, tube-like tongues. They store this nectar in their honey stomachs, where enzymes begin to break down the sugars. Upon returning to the hive, worker bees regurgitate the nectar into the mouths of other workers, passing it along until most of the water content evaporates. The result is honey, a highly nutritious and long-lasting food source.

Throughout history, humans have developed various methods to harvest honey, from simple clay pots used by ancient civilizations to modern-day beekeeping techniques. Honey has remained a valuable commodity due to its versatility and unique properties. It not only serves as a natural sweetener but also possesses antiseptic and medicinal qualities. In fact, honey has been used to treat wounds, coughs, and sore throats for centuries.

In summary, bees have been an integral part of human history, culture, and survival. From ancient civilizations to modern times, their remarkable societal structure, pollination abilities, and honey production have shaped human civilization. While bees face challenges in the modern world, efforts to protect and preserve them continue. Bees are not simply insects; they are a testament to the wonders of nature and the interconnectedness between humans and the natural world.

CHAPTER 10

Bees in Pop Culture

Bees have not only become a beloved part of our natural world but have also made their way into popular culture through various forms of media, providing entertainment and even education. From cartoons to movies to music, bees have become iconic and recognizable symbols that capture the imagination of people of all ages.

One of the most prevalent and amusing examples of bees in pop culture is found in the world of children's entertainment. Children's cartoons and shows often feature lively and endearing bee characters, delighting young viewers with their buzzing personalities. For instance, the classic animated series "Maya the Bee" follows the adventures of a curious and adventurous young bee named Maya. Her mischievous nature and eagerness to explore the world beyond her hive make for entertaining and educational storytelling that engages children while also imparting valuable lessons about friendship, teamwork, and the importance of bees in our ecosystem. As Maya navigates her way through exciting escapades, children not only get entertained but also learn about the important role bees play in pollination and honey production, fostering a sense of appreciation and respect for these tiny insects.

Moving beyond the realm of animation, bees have also made their mark in liveaction movies. The 2008 film "The Secret Life of Bees," based on the best-selling novel by Sue Monk Kidd, weaves a poignant and inspiring tale about a young girl on a journey of self-discovery, intertwined with the world of beekeeping. Through heartwarming storytelling, the film sheds light on the nurturing and transformative power of bees, offering a deeper understanding of the incredible bond that humans can form with these small creatures. The bees in the movie serve as a metaphor for growth, resilience, and the interconnectedness of all living beings, resonating with audiences and highlighting the importance of empathy and connection.

Bees have also found their way into the world of music, inspiring musicians to incorporate them into their compositions. From playful references to more profound symbolism, bees have become a recurring theme in songs across various genres. For instance, the iconic band Queen rocked the charts with their hit song "Killer Queen," which features the line, "She keeps her Moët et Chandon in her pretty cabinet, 'Let them eat cake,' she says, just like Marie Antoinette." This clever nod to bees is a pun on the phrase "let them eat cake" and highlights the queen bee's glamorous and powerful persona, capturing the imagination of listeners.

Furthermore, bees' influence in music extends beyond just lyrics; they have even inspired entire musical genres. In the 1990s, a vibrant subculture called "Bee Pop" emerged, characterized by catchy melodies, honey-sweet harmonies, and lyrics centered around themes of nature, unity, and social change. Bee Pop artists, such as The Bee Gees, The Bee-tles, and The Honey Bunch, brought joy and positivity to the airwaves, creating a buzz among listeners with their bee-themed music. The contagious energy and optimism infused in Bee Pop not only entertained but also served as a gentle reminder of the importance of environmental awareness and conservation.

In addition to their presence in children's shows, movies, and music, bees have also been immortalized in various forms of merchandise. From cute bee-themed t-shirts and toys to household items like bee-shaped honey pots and bee-printed kitchen accessories, bees have become a popular and fashionable motif. This trend not only showcases the enduring appeal of bees in pop culture but also serves as a reminder of our collective responsibility to protect these invaluable creatures.

In conclusion, bees have infiltrated pop culture in various forms, leaving an indelible mark on entertainment and storytelling. Through cartoons, movies, music, and merchandise, bees have captured our imagination and brought important messages about environmental conservation, interconnectedness, and the wonders of the natural world into our lives. As we continue to celebrate bees in popular culture, let us remember the vital role they play in sustaining our ecosystem and strive to protect and preserve them for generations to come.

CHAPTER 11

Bees in Science Fiction

Bees have always captured the imagination of authors and filmmakers, leading to their inclusion in a wide range of science fiction works. From futuristic societies to intergalactic adventures, bees have been reimagined and given exciting roles in these fictional worlds.

In some science fiction stories, bees are depicted as highly intelligent beings capable of communication and complex tasks. They are often portrayed as having their own societies and hierarchies, mirroring human civilization in a miniature form. These intelligent bees are shown to possess a collective consciousness, making group decisions and working together toward common goals. The intricate social structure of honeybee colonies, with their division of labor and communication through dance, offers a rich source of inspiration for writers and filmmakers when creating these imaginative bee societies.

Other science fiction tales take a more imaginative approach, incorporating futuristic technologies and concepts. Bees in these stories might be genetically modified or enhanced with advanced capabilities, such as being able to navigate through space or carry out specific missions. Scientists and inventors within these fictional worlds have harnessed the incredible adaptability and skills of bees to develop them as versatile tools. These augmented bees can aid in tasks like surveillance, search and rescue missions, or even serve as bioengineered messengers in interstellar travels.

In some instances, bees are used as symbols or metaphors in science fiction. They may represent harmony and balance in the natural world, contrasting with a dystopian or post-apocalyptic setting. Through these portrayals, authors explore the potential consequences of environmental degradation and the importance of preserving nature. Bees, with their role as pollinators, can symbolize the disruption or restoration of ecosystems, reflecting deeper environmental themes prevalent in these stories. They serve as a poignant reminder of the fragile interdependence between humans and their surrounding environment.

One famous example of bees in science fiction can be found in the novel and subsequent movie adaptation, "The Bees" by Laline Paull. Set in a dystopian future, the story revolves around a beehive and its inhabitants, with the bees serving as both characters and a metaphor for societal structures. Through their experiences and struggles, the novel explores themes of identity, power, and conformity. The author cleverly weaves together the intricate lives of bees with human-like emotions and complex relationships, epitomizing the merging of science fiction and social commentary.

Another notable mention is the "Bee Ship" from the science fiction TV series, "Doctor Who." This spaceship, shaped like a giant bee, is piloted by the insectoid species known as the Zarbi. The Bee Ship and the Zarbi add an element of mystery and otherworldliness to the show, showcasing how bees can be incorporated into science fiction as both fascinating creatures and intriguing plot devices. The inclusion of bees in the Doctor Who universe provides a captivating juxtaposition of the familiar (bees) and the unfamiliar (space travel and alien lifeforms), making the narrative both accessible and engaging.

Bees in science fiction serve to ignite our imagination, pushing the boundaries of what is possible and challenging our perceptions of the natural world. Whether they are presented as sentient beings, futuristic tools, or symbols of a dystopian future, bees add an element of wonder and fascination to the genre.

As we delve deeper into the realms of science fiction, it becomes evident that bees have become an integral part of the diverse and imaginative universe created by authors and filmmakers. Through their presence, bees showcase the boundless creativity and the ability to transform the ordinary into the extraordinary that defines the genre of science fiction. Their inclusion sparks discussions about the potential technological advancements and moral dilemmas that could arise from manipulating nature, as well as the value of preserving the delicate ecosystems upon which our world relies.

Moreover, the portrayal of bees in science fiction has not been limited to serious and thought-provoking themes alone. There have been instances where bees have been featured for their comedic appeal, providing lighthearted and amusing moments for audiences, including kids.

In animated movies and children's books, bees have been given charming and laughter-inducing characterizations. They often possess goofy personalities or engage in comical mishaps, adding a whimsical touch to the narratives. These humorous portrayals of bees not only entertain young readers and viewers but also contribute to their understanding and appreciation of these vital insects in a fun and engaging way.

Take, for example, the animated film, "Bee Movie." Released in 2007, this delightful comedy adventure follows the story of Barry B. Benson, a bee who ventures outside the hive and discovers the world of humans. Through witty dialogue and clever visual humor, the movie cleverly explores the relationship between bees and humans while also providing a delightful and hilarious experience for audiences of all ages.

In the world of children's literature, there are numerous funny bee stories that tickle young readers' funny bones. These stories often feature bees as mischievous characters who find themselves in amusing predicaments or embark on hilarious escapades. These tales use humor to engage children, making them laugh while also instilling a sense of curiosity and appreciation for the natural world.

From science fiction novels exploring bees' complex societies to animated movies and funny children's stories, bees continue to captivate us with their versatility and ability to transcend genres. They are woven into the fabric of science fiction with depth, imagination, and humor, reminding us of the multiplicity of ways in which these fascinating creatures can be represented.

So, whether you are embarking on a thrilling science fiction adventure, looking for a thought-provoking exploration of environmental themes, or seeking a good laugh, bees in science fiction have something to offer everyone. They present us with a captivating blend of the fantastical and the familiar, expanding our horizons and inviting us to explore the boundless possibilities that lie within the vast cosmos of science fiction.

CHAPTER 12

Bees in Digital Realms

In recent times, the influence of digital technology has permeated various aspects of our lives, including our fascination with bees. Bees, the industrious pollinators of the natural world, have found their way into the virtual realm, captivating both children and adults with their presence in video games, animated films, educational apps, and even digital artwork.

One particular genre of games that has embraced the idea of bees is the simulation genre. Players can step into the role of a beekeeper, managing their own virtual apiary and tending to the needs of their buzzing inhabitants. These games often provide players with an educational experience, teaching them about bee behavior, honey production, and the importance of conservation. Players can embark on missions, collecting pollen, avoiding predators, and even racing against time to pollinate flowers and save their hive. It's truly remarkable how these digital simulations offer a glimpse into the life of a beekeeper, allowing players to feel the thrill of the hive without the risk of getting stung!

Beyond simulations, bees have also made appearances in popular video games as supporting characters or plot devices. Their inclusion adds an extra layer of realism to these virtual worlds. In some games, players may encounter quests or missions centered around helping beleaguered bees or solving puzzles by imitating their behavior. Imagine exploring fantastical realms, conquering challenges, all while collaborating with digital bees as your trusty companions! These games not only entertain but also spark curiosity about the vital role bees play in our ecosystem.

In the realm of animated films, bees have become iconic characters in their own right. From the heartwarming tale of "Bee Movie" to the delightful adventures in the "Maya the Bee" series, these films have captured the imaginations of children and adults alike. Through colorful animation and entertaining storylines, these movies not only entertain but also help foster an appreciation for the significance of bees in our world. They cleverly combine humor and adventure, making audiences laugh while subtly imparting important ecological lessons. After all, who can resist a punny bee joke or a comically clumsy bee character? These movies offer a delightful blend of entertainment and education, ensuring that both kids and adults leave the theater both entertained and informed.

Educational apps have also seized the opportunity to educate children about bees in engaging ways. These digital tools provide interactive learning experiences, teaching about topics such as bee anatomy, life cycles, and the intricate process of pollination. With colorful graphics and playful characters, these apps capture children's attention, making learning about bees an enjoyable experience. They can explore virtual gardens, engaging in fun activities like guiding bees to flowers or collecting nectar. Children can interact with these digital bees, learning how to make their own nectar, or even giggle at funny bee jokes during educational quizzes. These apps not only teach but also inspire young minds to become future advocates for bee conservation. By making learning about bees fun and memorable, they contribute to raising awareness about their importance.

In the world of digital media, bees have not only provided entertainment and education but have also become the subject of creative endeavors. Artists have taken inspiration from bees to create visually stunning digital artwork showcasing their beauty and intricacy. Through digital paintings, illustrations, and even virtual reality experiences, we can immerse ourselves in the mesmerizing world of bees like never before. Virtual reality experiences take us on an extraordinary journey, where we can witness the intricate dance of bees communicating, explore vibrant digital flowers, and perhaps even share a laugh with a bee telling a funny joke. These digital artworks not only celebrate the magnificence of bees but also serve as a reminder of their vital role in our ecosystems.

The presence of bees in digital realms serves as a testament to the enduring fascination with these tiny creatures. Whether they are buzzing around in video games, enchanting us in animated films, teaching us about their amazing abilities through educational apps, or featured in digital artwork, bees continue to capture our imagination and remind us of their vital role in our world.

They offer us humor and laughter, while also highlighting the importance of conservation and the interconnectedness of our digital and natural worlds. So, as we venture into the ever-expanding digital realms, let us not forget the humble yet extraordinary bees and the enduring lessons they teach us about nature, teamwork, and the marvels of the interconnected world we live in.

CHAPTER 13

Fun Facts about Bees

Did you know that bees have been around for millions of years? These remarkable insects have captivated the attention of scientists and bee enthusiasts alike for centuries. In this chapter, we will explore some fascinating and lighthearted facts about bees that are sure to put a smile on your face.

1. Bees are excellent dancers:

Yes, you read that right! Bees communicate with each other through a series of intricate dances known as the "waggle dance." This dance is not only a form of communication but also a dance-off! Bees compete to see who can perform the most mesmerizing waggle dance, with the winner earning the title of the "Grooviest Bee in the Colony." They even have a panel of bee judges who rate their dance moves based on enthusiasm, creativity, and rhythm.

2. Bees are master architects:

When it comes to building their homes, bees have an impressive talent for architecture. The hexagonal shape of their honeycombs not only allows for efficient storage of honey, pollen, and eggs but also creates a mesmerizing optical illusion. Bees love to have fun with their chosen housing design and often play pranks on unsuspecting bees by making the honeycombs appear to sway and spin! They even have competitions to see who can create the most mind-bending honeycomb illusion, leaving their fellow bees in awe.

3. Bees have their own social hierarchy:

Within a bee colony, there is a structured hierarchy. However, even bees enjoy a good joke every now and then. The worker bees often play "Hide and Seek" with the queen bee, pretending to be lost and making her search for them. This playful activity helps strengthen their bond and create a fun-filled atmosphere within the hive. The queen bee, being an expert hider, occasionally disguises herself as a lowly worker bee to trick her subjects, resulting in fits of giggles when the truth is revealed.

4. Bees are great at teamwork:

Bees exemplify the power of teamwork. When a forager bee discovers a new food source, it returns to the hive and communicates the location to other bees through the waggle dance. However, bees also enjoy some friendly competition during their food-gathering missions. They challenge each other to races, competing to bring back the most pollen and nectar within a given time frame. The winner receives a special buzzing badge of honor! And in a true spirit of camaraderie, the bees organize celebratory picnics after each race, sharing their gathered treats and engaging in honey-tasting competitions.

5. Bees can recognize human faces:

Believe it or not, bees are capable of recognizing individual human faces. In addition to this remarkable ability, bees enjoy putting on a show for their human friends. Whenever a new face is introduced, the bees organize a grand aerial spectacle, forming intricate shapes and patterns in the air, as if to say, "Welcome, new friend!" They use their vibrant colors and synchronized movements to create beautiful displays that delight both young and old.

6. Bees are not all about honey:

While honey is undoubtedly a beloved product of bees, it is not the only thing they produce. Beeswax, apart from its various uses in cosmetics, candles, and polish, is also the secret ingredient bees use for making their signature "Bee Balm" lip balm, which keeps their lips soft and buzzing all day long. They even share this lip balm with other insects to ensure everyone has smooth, fluttery lips! Bees also have a talent for fashion and create intricate outfits by weaving together flower petals and leaves. These outfits are showcased during their seasonal fashion shows, where bees strut the runway in style.

7. Bees are incredibly hard workers:

A single honeybee will visit thousands of flowers in its lifetime, collecting nectar and pollen. But bees understand the importance of taking breaks and having some fun too. After a long day of foraging, they gather together for a buzzing choir concert, where each bee showcases its unique buzztastic talent, creating a symphony of sweet sounds that can be heard throughout the whole hive. They even invite other buzzing creatures like grasshoppers and cicadas to join in, creating harmonies that make the flowers sway and the trees dance. These are just a few fun facts about bees that highlight their remarkable abilities and unique characteristics. They are truly incredible creatures that continue to inspire awe and fascination. So, the next time you see a bee buzzing by, imagine the hidden laughter in their waggle dances, the joyous moments they share within their vibrant colonies,and the hilarious adventures they embark on in their buzzing world.

GLOSSARY

Glossary

1. Apiary:

A place where beehives are kept; a beekeeper's hive collection.

2. Bee Bread:

A special mixture of pollen and nectar that worker bees feed to the larvae.

3. Bee Dance (Waggle Dance):

A dance-like movement by bees to communicate the location of food sources.

4. Beekeeper:

A person who cares for and manages bee colonies.

5. Beeswax:

A substance produced by bees to build their hive and create honeycomb cells.

6. Biodiversity:

The variety of life in the world or in a particular habitat or ecosystem.

7. Colony:

A group of bees living together, typically consisting of a queen, worker bees, and drones.

8. Compound Eyes:

Large eyes on bees made up of thousands of tiny lenses.

9. Drones:

Male bees whose primary role is to mate with the queen.

10. Ecosystem:

A biological community of interacting organisms and their physical environment.

11. Habitat:

The natural home or environment of an animal, plant, or other organism.

12. Honey:

A sweet substance made by bees from nectar.

13. Honeycomb:

A structure of hexagonal cells made by bees for storing honey and eggs

14. Hymenoptera:

The order of insects that includes bees, wasps, and ants.

15. Larvae:

The immature form of bees, before they develop into adults.

16. Nectar:

A sweet liquid secreted by flowers, collected by bees to make honey.

17. Ocelli:

Small, simple eyes on bees used for detecting light intensity.

18. Pollen:

Fine powdery substance produced by flowers, collected by bees for food.

19. Pollination:

The transfer of pollen from male to female parts of plants, often facilitated by bees.

20. Proboscis:

A long, straw-like tongue on bees for collecting nectar.

21. Queen Bee:

The female leader of a bee colony, responsible for laying eggs.

22. Royal Jelly:

A nutrient-rich substance fed to queen larvae and adult queens.

23. Species:

A group of living organisms consisting of similar individuals capable of exchanging genes.

24. Stinger:

A sharp organ in bees used for defense, present only in females.

25. Worker Bees:

Female bees who perform various tasks like collecting food and maintaining the hive.

ABOUT US

About Us

The Bug Collective, founded by a dad and his two sons, is an inspiring family venture rooted in a shared passion for the fascinating world of insects.

Born from a simple backyard exploration, their interest in bugs blossomed into a creative endeavor. They aim to craft engaging and informative books about the entomological wonders they discover.

Through their work, they seek to ignite curiosity and foster a deeper appreciation for the intricate lives of bugs in readers young and old. The Bug Collective is more than a publishing venture; it's a celebration of nature's tiny marvels, brought to you by a family that finds joy in every creepy crawler and fluttering wing.